THE MUMM[Y'S] MISSING WR[AP]

DINESH DECKKER
SUBHASHINI SUMANASEKARA

First Published in 2024 IN USA

ISBN-13 : 9798342469258

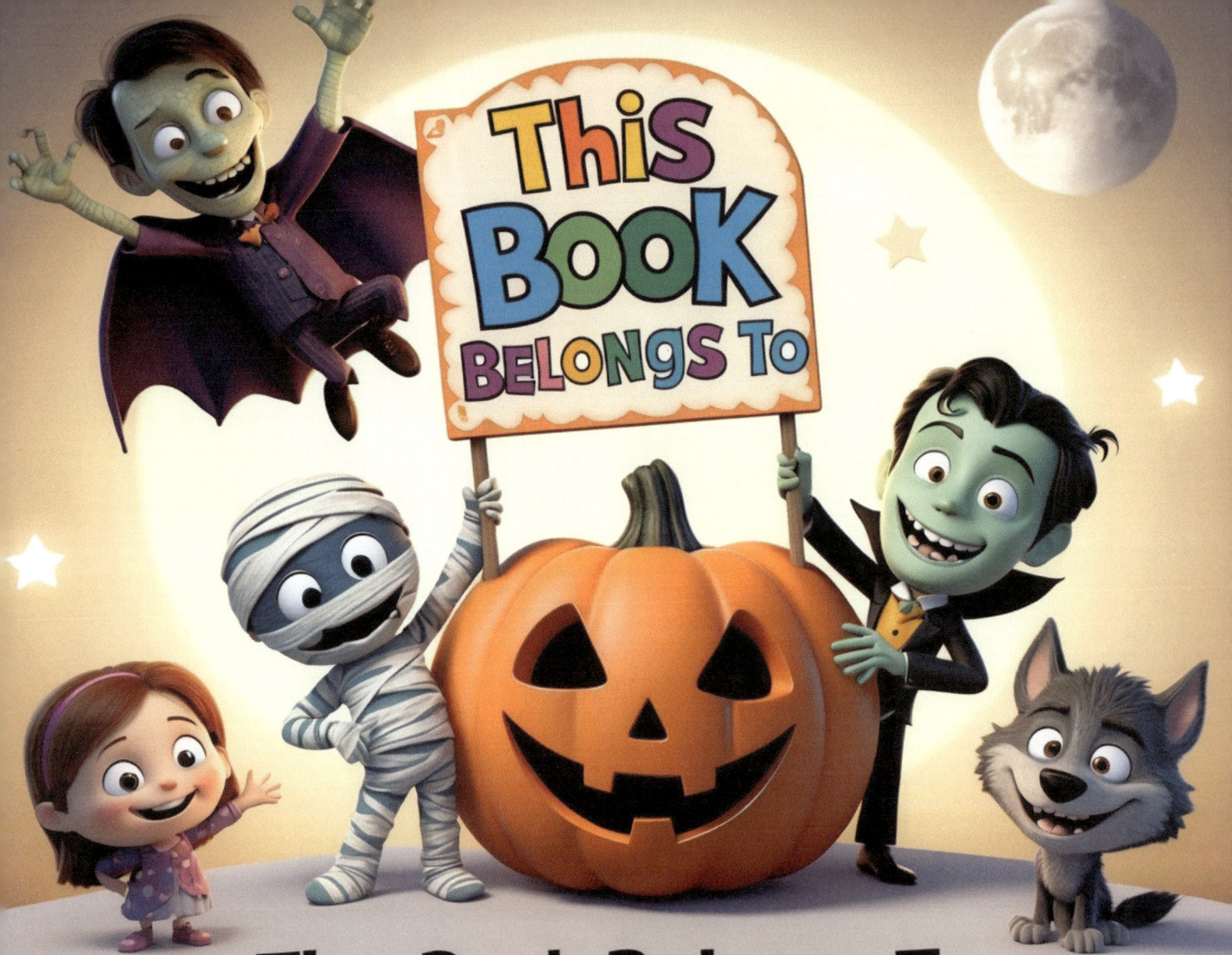

This Book Belongs To

Introduction

Marvin the mummy is excited for Halloween night—until he discovers that something is missing! Feeling embarrassed, he hides away while his friends, Victor the vampire, Wally the werewolf, and Zara the zombie, set off on a spooky quest. Will they be able to find what's missing and bring Marvin back to the party? Join them on this fun adventure to find out!

Marvin the mummy woke up on Halloween night.

"Oh no!" he cried.
"I'm missing half my wraps!"

Marvin hid behind a tree, feeling too shy to join the party.

"What if everyone laughs at me?" he thought.

His friends—Victor the vampire, Wally the werewolf, and Zara the zombie—noticed he was missing.

"Where's Marvin?" asked Zara.

They found Marvin hiding behind the tree.

"What's wrong, Marvin?" asked Victor.

"I'm missing half my bandages," Marvin whispered.

"I can't go to the party like this."

"Don't worry, we'll help you find them!" said Wally.

"We're in this together," Zara added with a smile.

They searched the old graveyard.

"There's nothing here
but dusty bones!" laughed Wally.

Next, they searched the haunted house.

"Only cobwebs and creaky floors!" said Victor.

Then, they heard a soft "whoosh" in the wind.

"Look, it's a bandage stuck in that tree!" shouted Zara.

They followed the trail of bandages through the forest.

"There's more over here!" called Victor.

Finally, they gathered all of Marvin's wraps.

"We found them all, Marvin!" said Wally.

Marvin wrapped himself up again, feeling happy.

"Thanks, friends. I realized you liked me just the way I am!"

Message from the Story:

Marvin learned that true friends love you for who you are, not how you look. They'll always be there to help, no matter what. Remember, you are special just the way you are, and with friends by your side, you can face any adventure!

DINESH DECKKER

AUTHOR

Dinesh Deckker is a multifaceted author and educator with a rich academic background and extensive experience in creative writing and education. Holding a BSc Hons in Computer Science, a BA (Hons), and an MBA from prestigious institutions in the UK, Dinesh has dedicated his career to blending technology, education, and literature.

BA, MBA (UK),PhD (Student)

He has further honed his writing skills through a variety of specialized courses. His qualifications include:

- Children Acquiring Literacy Naturally from UC Santa Cruz, USA
- Creative Writing Specialization from Wesleyan University, USA
- Writing for Young Readers Commonwealth Education Trust
- Introduction to Early Childhood from The State University of New York
- Introduction to Psychology from Yale University
- Academic English: Writing Specialization University of California, Irvine,
- Writing and Editing Specialization from University of Michigan
- Writing and Editing: Word Choice University of Michigan
- Sharpened Visions: A Poetry Workshop from CalArts, USA
- Grammar and Punctuation from University of California, Irvine, USA
- Teaching Writing Specialization from Johns Hopkins University
- Advanced Writing from University of California, Irvine, USA
- English for Journalism from University of Pennsylvania, USA
- Creative Writing: The Craft of Character from Wesleyan University, USA
- Creative Writing: The Craft of Setting from Wesleyan University
- Creative Writing: The Craft of Plot from Wesleyan University, USA
- Creative Writing: The Craft of Style from Wesleyan University, USA

Dinesh's diverse educational background and commitment to lifelong learning have equipped him with a deep understanding of various writing styles and educational techniques. His works often reflect his passion for storytelling, education, and technology, making him a versatile and engaging author.

SUBHASHINI SUMANASEKARA
AUTHOR

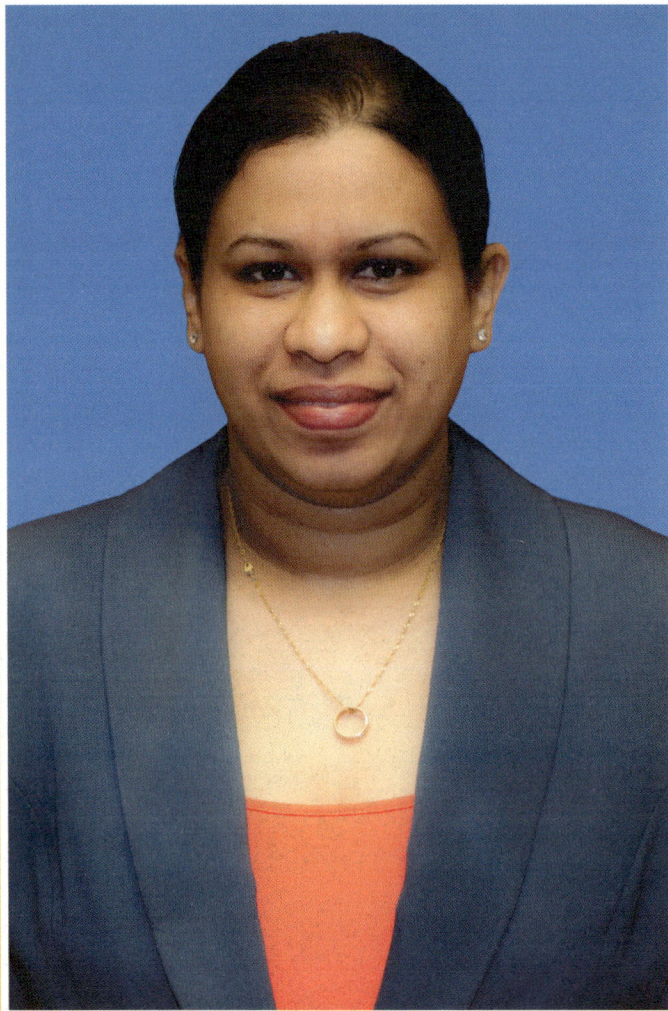

With more than 20 years of expertise, Subhashini Sumanasekara is a renowned ICT educator committed to mentoring students from a variety of backgrounds. Her experience in the industry is further enhanced by her Master of Science in Strategic IT Management.

BSc, MSc (UK), PhD (Student)

Printed in Dunstable, United Kingdom